12 WAYS TO STAY
ACTIVE AND FIT

by Jamie Kallio

Run for Cardio Fitness

One of the best ways to stay active and fit is to take part in cardiovascular exercise, or cardio. Cardio is good for the body in many ways. It makes your heart and lungs strong. It keeps your blood pumping through your body. Running is a form of cardio. It has many health benefits. Running improves the function of a person's heart, blood vessels, and lungs. Many runners set running goals. They feel accomplished after meeting those goals. Running can be done almost anywhere. You can run outside or on a treadmill or an indoor track. Many runners don't let rain or snow stop them.

It is safe for kids as young as eight years old to run up to three miles (4.8 km). Whether you run one mile or three, be sure to give yourself plenty of walk breaks. Wearing the right kind of shoes is also important. Good shoes will go a long way in

Stretch before and after running.

While running, sip some water every 15 to 20 minutes to stay hydrated.

preventing falls. Remember good posture when running. Feet should always be placed directly under the hips. Another thing to avoid is bending at the waist while running. Running this way is bad for your leg muscles.

Before setting out on a run, be sure to warm up with dynamic stretches. Dynamic stretching includes high knee raises and walking lunges. Have a small snack 30 minutes before you go on a run. This will help keep up your energy. After your run, walk to let your muscles cool down. Gently stretch any tight areas. Be sure to keep hydrated even after you finish your run.

46 million
Number of running shoes sold in the United States in 2013.

- Running helps strengthen the cardiovascular system.
- Maintaining good posture and keeping hydrated are important tips for running.
- Do some dynamic stretching before every run.

HISTORY OF THE MARATHON

The length of a marathon is 26.2 miles (42 km). This is in honor of the Greek soldier Pheidippides who lived in 490 BCE. At that time, Athens was at war with the Persians. When the Persians were defeated, Pheidippides ran from the city of Marathon, Greece, to Athens to tell of the victory. The run was just less than 26 miles long. When Pheidippides reached Athens, he cried, "Niki!" which means "victory!"

Improve Body and Mind with Hiking

Hiking is another form of cardio and a good way to stay fit. And it's fun and adventurous. Hiking lets you enjoy nature. You can choose a route and make the hike as challenging as you want. When first starting out, it is a good idea not to tackle a difficult trail. Start with a short, simple trail. Beginner trails have an easier terrain. They don't have as many hills or obstacles. You can build up your hiking experience over time.

Depending on the terrain and weather, you can choose between hiking sandals or hiking boots. Dress for the weather. Wear clothes that protect against the wind and wear layers that you can take off if you get too warm. Also bring along hats and gloves in case the weather turns chilly or too sunny. Bring along

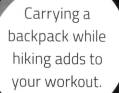

Carrying a backpack while hiking adds to your workout.

Drink water often throughout your hike to keep your body hydrated.

snacks and water so you can refuel your body during your hike. It is best not to hike alone. Always hike with friends or family. Carrying a backpack full of gear adds to your workout. It strengthens your muscles and bones. This is because carrying extra weight puts extra stress on muscles and bones. Over time, you will grow stronger.

Another benefit of hiking is the good it can do for a person's mind. Research has shown that everyone needs to get outdoors for his or her health and well-being. Going on a hike and experiencing nature boosts your mood and mind. Being outdoors also improves creativity.

29 million

Number of people in the United States who went hiking in 2015.

- Hiking will strengthen your bones because it is a weight-bearing exercise.
- Know the terrain and weather so that you know how to dress.
- Being outdoors is necessary for a person's well-being.

THINK ABOUT IT

Hiking can be done almost anywhere, but many people like to use trails in national or regional parks. Using another source, look up how many parks are in your area. Can you find how many of them offer hiking trails?

Get a Total Body Workout with Swimming

Swimming is a fun and easy way to stay fit and to exercise many of your body's muscles. Biceps, triceps, and hamstrings are worked. Your arms, legs, and core will all grow strong from swimming. Swimming is a low-impact sport. This means it is easy on your joints. Since it is low-impact, many people exercise longer when in a pool.

There is another bonus to swimming. Learning to swim can prevent drowning. The earlier in life you take swimming lessons, the safer you will be in the water.

Swimming in lakes and other bodies of water is a favorite outdoor activity on hot days. There are many indoor pools where you can swim any time

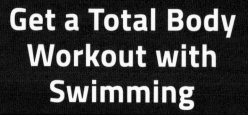

Many muscles work together as you push and pull your way through the water.

of the year. Many health clubs offer the use of indoor pools. Indoor swimming is an activity you can do alone or with a team. Some schools also have swimming pools. You could try joining a swim team.

Some people use goggles to protect their eyes when swimming underwater. Others wear earplugs and nose clips to keep water out. If you want to dive, make sure the water in the pool is deep enough. When swimming outdoors, put on water-resistant sunscreen to prevent sunburns.

25
Standard number of yards in one lap of a swimming pool.

- Swimming is a low-impact sport.
- Swimming can be an individual activity or a team sport.
- Try joining a swim team, or just swim on your own.

Having fun with friends while swimming is an easy way to exercise.

Learn Balance through Biking

Bicycling can give you a sense of freedom and adventure and improve your mood. Every time you hit the pedals, you are also helping your body. Riding a bike develops strength in the lower legs. It also builds balance.

You know that when you bike, you have to pump the pedals. You also have to balance, steer, and think about speed. When riding, you have to make adjustments to how you sit, stand, and push the pedals. All of these skills help you learn and maintain balance. You can bike for sport or for fun. Instead of riding in a car, bike if the distance isn't too far. Stick to paths you know, and try not to ride alone.

Biking is a low-impact exercise, so there is minimal strain on your knees and joints.

Wear brightly colored clothes when biking so that you are visible to cars.

There are some safety issues to consider when biking. Wear a helmet every time you ride. A helmet will protect your head if you fall or crash. Wear shoes that can grip the bike's pedals. This means no flip-flops. And just as if you were in a car, obey all traffic rules. Stop at stop signs and red lights. Obey crosswalk rules. Walk your bike across a busy intersection. Avoid listening to music on earphones or being distracted by a smartphone. Finally, try to have your bike tuned up once a year at a bike shop.

1817

Year that the bicycle was introduced to the world by German inventor, Karl Drais.

- Riding a bike requires the use of many skills at once, such as balancing, pedaling, and steering.
- Wear a helmet every time you ride your bike.
- Bicyclers should obey all traffic signals just as they would in a vehicle.

Dance to Break a Sweat

You can break a sweat and fit in a workout while hanging out with friends. Dancing, whether alone or with friends, is fun and doesn't seem like exercise. From ballet to hip hop, dancing provides many opportunities for fun fitness. You get to choose the music. And the movement in dancing is always changing, making it a great cardio workout. It also helps to improve memory. There are usually steps and dance patterns to remember while dancing. You and your friends can learn new dance routines together. Or you can just dance around any way you want.

Some people take professional dance classes. Since it is a

Dancing as a form of exercise can be as simple as free-form dancing with your friends.

physically demanding activity, dancers gain increased muscle strength and coordination. Dancing can even help correct poor posture. Dance lessons are a great way to make new friends. Whether you are on a dance team or perform alone, you will be around other people who love the same exercise. If you are on a team, you will learn teamwork and coordination. No matter what form of dance you choose, your sense of focus and discipline will improve. These are skills that can carry over into other areas of your life, such as schoolwork.

1902
Year the first contemporary dance was performed by American Isadora Duncan.

- Dancing is a great cardio workout that also improves memory.
- Dancing is a highly demanding activity.
- The focus learned in dancing will carry over to other areas of your life.

Regular dance practice will help improve your flexibility, strength, and endurance.

Join a Sport to Increase Endurance

Regular exercise keeps us active and fit. It gives us energy, helps control weight, and can even help us live longer. Participating in a sport will help you increase your endurance and give you stronger muscles and bones. There are many sports to choose from. If you enjoy team sports, you may like basketball for its high intensity. All the running, dribbling, and jumping will build up your endurance. The most popular team sports in the United States are basketball, baseball or softball, football, and soccer.

Soccer is a popular, high-energy team sport that increases endurance.

EAT TO BE FIT

Playing sports is one way to stay fit. Eating right is equally important. Be sure to eat plenty of fruits and vegetables. Quality protein—in the form of foods such as meat, fish, and eggs—should also be part of your meals, as well as whole grains. Reach for water or juice instead of soda for your drinks. Keep your body well fueled so you can feel and play your best.

THINK ABOUT IT

Are you involved in any sports or personal physical activity? If so, which ones do you prefer? How have they helped you become stronger? What are some other sports you want to try?

36 million

Number of kids in the United States who play in organized sports each year.

- Participating in sports increases endurance.
- There are many team sports and individual sports to choose from.
- Always be cleared by a doctor before playing any sport.

You don't have to join a team to be involved in a sport. There are individual sports and activities, such as snowboarding and kayaking. Kayaking is a challenging upper body workout. Continued use of upper body muscles will help increase overall endurance.

Being involved in any kind of competitive sport teaches you how to compete in a friendly and safe environment. Sports require regular practice. This helps you improve your skills. It also helps strengthen your body. Most importantly, playing sports is a fun way to spend your time. Before playing any sport, you should have a physical exam by a doctor. This will ensure that you are healthy enough for a particular sport.

Being a part of a team is a great way to meet new friends.

15

Exercise Anywhere with Jump Ropes

Maybe you're not interested in joining a specific sport but still want to be active on your own. One easy way to do this is by jumping rope. Jump ropes are inexpensive to buy. Your jump rope can be either a lightweight one bought at a toy store or a plastic one bought from a sporting goods store. Both kinds work equally well. Jump ropes are also small, so they're easy to store and carry around. Use it in the living room while watching television. Bring it to school and use it during recess or free periods. Whether you use it indoors or out, your jump rope is always ready to go.

Jumping rope works your heart and tones your muscles. It also improves coordination. You have to focus on your feet jumping in time with the rope. The more you practice, the more coordinated you will be. If you play other sports, jumping rope can help prevent foot and ankle injuries. It strengthens the muscles in the ankles and feet. Jump rope to warm up before playing other sports, such as basketball, or to cool down after a run or bike ride.

You can jump rope alone or with friends. Challenge each other to learn tricks

You can jump rope almost anywhere.

Compete with friends to see who can jump the highest or lowest. You can even try spinning while jumping rope.

or double Dutch. In double Dutch, two long ropes turn in opposite directions. The jumpers have to time out both ropes. There are many chants you can learn while you jump to help keep the rhythm.

AN ANCIENT FORM

Ancient Egyptians used vines to jump and play. Medieval paintings show children jumping rope. Eventually jumping rope spread from Egypt to Europe and finally to North America. Dutch settlers in the United States were some of the first to jump rope in the Americas. One of the most popular jump rope games is called double Dutch.

10
Minutes of jumping rope that provides the same workout as an eight-minute one-mile (1.6 km) jog.

- Jump ropes are inexpensive and easy to carry around.
- The more you practice jumping rope, the lighter on your feet you will be.
- Jumping rope helps improve coordination and cardiovascular strength.

Strengthen Legs with Skating

Skating is an activity that can be done all year long. Inline skating and ice-skating are two popular types of skating. The difference between inline and ice-skating are the types of skates and the surface on which a person skates. Inline skates have four wheels that roll on hard, smooth surfaces such as sidewalks. Ice skates have a long blade and are meant to be used on ice. Sidewalks and trails are great for inline skating. Outdoor ice rinks are available in winter for ice-skating. Many towns have rinks for both inline and ice-skating.

The benefits of both types of skating include strong leg muscles and a strong core. Your body uses your core as you skate to help you keep your balance. Keeping your core strong also helps your posture. Inline skating can be great

Both ice-skating and inline skating build strong leg and core muscles.

- Both inline and ice-skating are year-round activities.
- Using your core as you skate improves your balance and posture.
- When choosing skates, make sure you find ones that provide strong ankle support.

Wear protective gear and make sure your skates fit properly.

off-season practice for hockey players, but anyone can do it just for fun. You can play roller hockey, go to a skate park, or just cruise down the sidewalk. Ice-skating can be done either outside on a skating pond or indoors on a rink.

For either activity, having the right safety equipment is important. Choose skates that give your ankles strong support. With inline skates, wear absorbent socks. With ice skates, wear thin socks for a good fit. Always wear a helmet to protect your head. Knee and elbow pads are helpful, too, in case of falls. Stretch your muscles for a light warm-up before skating.

Build Muscles by Skateboarding

Skateboarding is another great way to strengthen muscles. Quadriceps, or quads, are the large muscles at the front of your thighs. Out of all the muscles, your quads work the hardest while skateboarding. You and your quads can get a great workout just by skating in one direction. As you learn tricks, more muscles are used. For example, jumps and twists require your core to twist and turn. This builds strong abs. Since you use your eyes, legs, feet, abs, and arms when skateboarding, your coordination will improve.

While skateboarding can be an extreme sport, anyone can do it for fun. You can skateboard in a skate park or on skate trails. You can just skate up and down your driveway or street. Even skateboarding for fun takes practice and patience.

Many muscles are engaged while skateboarding.

Rubber-soled shoes help you grip the skateboard.

Once you learn how to skateboard, you might be able to easily learn other board sports such as surfing or snowboarding.

While learning to skateboard, remember these safety measures. It can be easy to lose your balance and fall at first. There are helmets made specifically for skateboarding. A helmet should always be worn when on a skateboard. Always wear closed-toe shoes with rubber soles. All beginners should start off with elbow and knee pads. Most importantly, use a skateboard that is the right size for you and the surfaces you plan to skate on.

4

Number of different deck styles to consider when choosing a skateboard: shortboard, cruiser, old school, or longboard.

- Skateboarding strengthens muscles, including the abs and quads.
- Learning to skateboard can help you learn other board sports such as surfing and snowboarding.
- Always wear a helmet when skateboarding, no matter how experienced you are.

21

Improve Focus with Martial Arts

Martial arts can strengthen both the mind and body. Popular forms of martial arts include karate, tae kwon do, kung fu, and aikido. Each form requires kicks, punches, and blocks. It takes a lot of practice and concentration to perform these skills. Since every muscle group in your body is used while practicing martial arts, it gives you a full body workout. Your muscles will lengthen and strengthen. Martial arts will also improve heart health and reflexes.

Classes run for about an hour and always begin with a warm-up.

Many people take martial arts for self-defense. However, martial arts are peaceful activities that improve discipline and develop focus. Part of martial arts is sitting quietly to develop stillness. Sitting still for a long period of time requires focus. Students also learn to listen to their bodies. Learning how to get in touch with your feelings and thoughts helps develop empathy for yourself and others. Respect is also

Martial arts hone your focus and muscles through strict training.

A statue in Hong Kong honors Bruce Lee and his contributions to martial arts.

very important in martial arts. Before any punching or kicking begins, every student bows to the master or instructor. Participants learn to treat the other students with kindness and fairness.

2000
Year that tae kwon do became an official Olympic sport.

- Many forms of martial arts require the student to learn kicks, punches, and blocks.
- Martial arts are best known for their lessons in self-discipline and focus.
- Learning respect is important in martial arts.

BRUCE LEE

Bruce Lee was a martial artist and film star born in San Francisco, California, in 1940. As a child, he starred in more than 20 films in Hong Kong. As an adult, he taught martial arts and developed a new style called jeet kune do. This style of martial arts incorporates moves from tae kwon do, wrestling, fencing, and boxing.

23

Exercise with Your Dog

Walking has plenty of health benefits. It strengthens the heart and improves mood. Experts say that owning a dog motivates people to exercise when they otherwise wouldn't. Most dogs need exercise to stay healthy and happy. They need it in good weather and bad. If you own a dog, it is your responsibility to make sure it is getting the exercise it needs. By walking your dog, you are also getting a good workout. Dog walking, and walking in general, can help fight off obesity.

There are other great reasons for walking a dog. Being outdoors with your dog helps to improve

Taking a dog for a walk or run benefits both you and the dog.

43 million

Number of people in the United States who owned a dog in 2012.

- Owning a dog motivates people to exercise more than they would without a dog.
- Dog walking and walking in general help fight obesity.
- If you cannot own a dog, ask to walk a neighbor or friend's dog.

THINK ABOUT IT

What other health benefits do pets provide for their owners? You already know that owning a dog helps people get out and walk more. Using other sources, find two or three more ways that owning a pet can help your health.

your attention and put you in a good mood. Studies have shown that playing with a dog provides a sense of calm and relaxation. It also helps your imagination. Training a dog to learn tricks can also be a great source of pride and accomplishment. If your family cannot own a dog, ask a neighbor if you can walk theirs. Maybe you can make a little extra money while you keep fit!

Throwing a Frisbee is another form of exercise that can incorporate a dog.

Boost Flexibility and Coordination with Yoga

Yoga is a lifelong activity that both young and old can take part in. It is an activity that can be practiced anywhere, with or without a mat. As long as you have a soft or smooth surface, you are ready to go!

Yoga combines mind, body, and spirit. Many forms of stretching and practiced breathing are used in yoga. Practiced breathing helps us to fully exhale old air out of our lungs. It also helps us to calm our minds and relax. Yoga requires a person to lie, stand, sit, and bend in different ways. This uses different groups of muscles. The repeated poses of yoga train the nervous system to let muscles stretch more. Being flexible helps prevent injury from other sports and in everyday life.

Balance and coordination are also practiced in yoga. The more you practice yoga, the more these skills will improve. Yoga also calls for focus. When you

Stretching your muscles repeatedly during yoga makes them longer.

In the downward dog yoga position, your body should make a triangular shape.

concentrate on breathing and hold a pose, you are improving your focus. With increased focus, you will be able to concentrate better in all areas of life, including at school.

Yoga is also a great way to let go of stress. Sometimes you might want a break from rushing around and being online or playing video games. In fact, the biggest benefits of all exercise are an improved mood, a healthy body, and a strong mind.

1.7 million

The number of children in the United States who practice yoga each year.

- Yoga can be practiced anywhere.
- The repeated stretching in yoga will make muscles more flexible.
- With practice, yoga will help to improve your focus.

EASY POSES FOR BEGINNERS

If you are just starting out with yoga, there are a few easy poses you can try. The first is the bridge pose. Lie on your back and bend both knees. Make sure your feet are flat on the ground. Then lift your hips to the sky. Another popular beginner pose is the downward dog. For this pose, start off on your hands and knees. Brace yourself with your hands and toes. Lift your bottom toward the ceiling.

Fact Sheet

- Kids between the ages of six and 16 need 60 minutes of exercise per day. Sixty minutes per day may seem like a lot at first, but exercise comes in many forms. Playing a sport, riding a bike, running a race with your friends, or doing jumping jacks while watching television are all forms of exercise. When you make exercise fun, you will be more likely to do it every day.

- One in three kids is obese. Childhood obesity can cause heart disease, high blood pressure, and asthma. Regular exercise can prevent childhood obesity and certain diseases. Exercise can build strong bones, improve your mindset, and help you focus in school. There are many organizations devoted to helping kids fight obesity. Let's Move is an organization created by First Lady Michelle Obama to help kids be healthy and happy. Let's Move teaches parents and kids how to make good food choices and how to get active.

- Participating in regular activity such as sports will help brain development. Exercise increases blood flow to the brain. Blood carries oxygen and glucose, which improve focus. Regular exercise also causes chemicals such as endorphins to increase. These chemicals improve mood and help to relieve stress. Research has shown that exercise improves the development of neurons. Neurons are cells that belong to the nervous system. They carry messages between the brain and other parts of the body.

Glossary

cardiovascular
Exercise that causes the heart to beat fast and hard for a period of time.

core
The muscles around the trunk and pelvis of the body.

double Dutch
The activity of jumping over two jump ropes held by two people. The ropes swing in opposite directions.

empathy
The ability to understand and share another person's feelings.

endurance
The ability to do something difficult for a long period of time.

obesity
A medical term that refers to having too much body fat.

posture
The way a body is positioned when sitting or standing.

terrain
The natural features of an outdoor setting.

For More Information

Books

Crockett, Kyle A. *Nutrition for Achievement in Sports and Academics.* Broomall, PA: Mason Crest, 2014.

Head, Honor. *Keeping Fit.* Mankato, MN: Sea-to-Sea Publications, 2013.

Hunt, Sara. *Stay Fit: Your Guide to Staying Active.* Mankato, MN: Capstone Press, 2012.

Visit 12StoryLibrary.com

Scan the code or use your school's login at **12StoryLibrary.com** for recent updates about this topic and a full digital version of this book. Enjoy free access to:

- Digital ebook
- Breaking news updates
- Live content feeds
- Videos, interactive maps, and graphics
- Additional web resources

Note to educators: Visit 12StoryLibrary.com/register to sign up for free premium website access. Enjoy live content plus a full digital version of every 12-Story Library book you own for every student at your school.

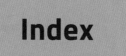

Index

About the Author

Jamie Kallio is a youth services librarian in the south suburbs of Chicago. She is the author of several nonfiction books for kids. When she is not writing or reading, she can be found playing with her Chihuahua mix puppy, Elsa.

READ MORE FROM 12-STORY LIBRARY

Every 12-Story Library book is available in many formats. For more information, visit 12StoryLibrary.com.